Reading My Bible in WINTER

LOU HEATH and BETH TAYLOR

BROADMAN PRESS
Nashville, Tennessee

Unless otherwise noted, Scripture quotations are from the King James Version of the Bible.

Scripture quotations marked (GNB) are from the *Good News Bible*, the Bible in Today's English Version. Old Testament: Copyright © American Bible Society 1976; New Testament: Copyright © American Bible Society 1966, 1971, 1976. Used by permission.

Scripture quotations marked (NASB) are from the *New American Standard Bible*. Copyright © The Lockman Foundation, 1960, 1962, 1963, 1968, 1971, 1972, 1973, 1975, 1977. Used by permission.

Scripture quotations marked (NIV) are from the HOLY BIBLE *New International Version*, copyright © 1978, New York Bible Society. Used by permission.

Library of Congress Cataloging-in-Publication Data

Heath, Lou Mishler.
  Reading my Bible in winter.

  Summary: A collection of devotional readings,
particularly appropriate for winter, including Bible
stories and verses, modern examples, questions, and
suggested activities.
  1. Children—Prayer-books and devotions—English.
[1. Prayer books and devotions] I. Taylor, Beth,
1938-   . II. Title.
BV4870.H39 1986   242'.2   85-30940
ISBN 0-8054-4323-1

To our grandchildren
with love and prayers

Dear Boys and Girls,

We have written this book especially for you. We hope you will begin to read your Bible everyday. The Bible is God's Word to you. It will help you know how God wants you to live and be happy.

Choose a special time of the day to read your Bible. Choose a quiet place to read your Bible.

Each page in this book lists a Bible passage to read. Some pages have puzzles or questions for you to think about and to do. Close this time with prayer.

Your Friends,

Mrs. Lou
Mrs. Beth

New Year

January 1

Read the Bible:

Locate and read Mark 12:28-34 in your Bible. Lightly color verses 30 and 31. "Love the Lord your God with all your heart, with all your soul, with all your mind, and with all your strength. The second most important commandment is this: Love your neighbor as you love yourself. There is no other commandment more important than these two" (GNB).

Think About This:

A teacher of the Law asked Jesus, "Which commandment is the most important of all?" What was Jesus' answer? Jesus said to "Love the Lord your God with:
1. all your _____
2. all your _____
3. all your _____
4. all your _____
Jesus also said to love your _____ as _____.

Pray Today:

Pray: "Heavenly Father, as this new year is just beginning, help me love You more than any person or any thing. Help me love others, and help me treat them just like I would like to be treated. I love You and want to please You. In Jesus' name, amen."

January 2

Read the Bible:

Read Ephesians 4:25-32. Do not hurry as you read. Underline Ephesians 4:32. Read this translation:
"Get rid of all bitterness, passion, and anger. No more shouting or insults, no more hateful feelings of any sort. Instead, be kind and tender-hearted to one another, and forgive one another, as God has forgiven you in Christ" (GNB).

Think About This:

Do you remember the story of the twin brothers, Jacob and Esau? Esau was very angry because his brother had tricked him. Twenty years later, Esau was able to forgive his brother. Think of all the years of hatred and anger.

God has promised to forgive us if we ask Him.

Pray Today:

Are you angry at anyone? Is there someone who has done something to you and you have not forgiven them? The beginning of this new year is a good time to be forgiving. Can you pray this prayer sincerely?

"Dear Father, I want to obey your words in the Bible. I want to forgive anyone who has done bad things to me. Help me think of anyone of whom I need to ask forgiveness. It does not feel good to be angry and unforgiving. I give this new year to You. Amen."

January 3

Read the Bible:

Locate and mark Proverbs 22:1 in your Bible. "A good name is to be more desired than great riches, Favor is better than silver and gold" (NASB).

Think About This:

We are known by the things we do. When we do good things, we honor God. Favor with God is worth more than anything money can buy.

Pray Today:

Pray: "Dear Father, help me do things to bring honor to Your name and to the name my parents gave to me. Help me want to please You. I know that one way to please You is to choose to obey my parents. Since this is the start of a new year, help me make good choices at school, at home, and at church. Amen."

January 4

Read the Bible:

Mark Joshua 1:9 in your Bible.
"Have I not commanded you? Be strong and coura-geous! Do not tremble or be dismayed, for the Lord your God is with you wherever you go" (NASB).

Think About This:

Knowing that God is with you can help you to be confident. Learning to make right choices is important. Making wrong choices can bring unhappy times at home and at church or at school with your friends. God will help you make right choices.

Pray Today:

Get a piece of paper and a pencil. Write out a prayer. Ask God to help you start the new year right. Ask God for courage to choose to do what is right and good in His sight.

January 5

Read the Bible:

Read Philippians 3:12-14.
"So I run straight toward the goal in order to win the prize, which is God's call through Christ Jesus to the life above" (GNB).

Think About This:

Paul, writing to the Philippian believers, wrote about aiming toward a goal. What did Paul say he was going to forget? _____. What "prize" was Paul talking about? _____ .

Do you have a goal in life? What would you like to do when you become an adult? What kind of work would you like to do? Where would you like to serve in church?

Would you be willing to be a missionary? Would you be willing to be a Christian businessman or businesswoman?

Pray Today:

Ask God to show you what you need to do for a vocation. Ask Him to help you set some goals. Ask Him to help you prepare for whatever He wants you to do.

January 6

Read the Bible:

Read 2 Timothy 3:14-17 in your Bible. Mark verse 15.
"You remember that ever since you were a child, you
have known the Holy Scriptures, which are able to give
you the wisdom that leads to salvation through faith in
Christ Jesus" (GNB).

Think About This:

Paul told Timothy the Holy Scriptures were useful
for five things. List them:

1.
2.
3.
4.
5.

Choosing Jesus Christ as your Savior will be the most
important thing you will ever do. Have you already
accepted Jesus? One of the best ways to grow as a Christian
is to read your Bible and to pray daily.

Pray Today:

Ask God for wisdom to know what His plan for your
life is. Ask Him to help you understand and remember
what the Bible teaches.

January 7

Read the Bible:

Read Psalm 23. Underline verse 1 and verse 6.
"Surely goodness and love will follow me all the days of my life, and I will dwell in the house of the Lord forever" (v. 6, NIV).

Think About This:

This is the favorite psalm of many people. You may not fully understand all that this psalm means. But as you read it and as you grow, it may become your favorite psalm.

David was a shepherd. He knew how important the shepherd was to the lambs. The shepherd protects the lambs. He sees that the lambs have food to eat and water to drink. He leads them through dangerous places. He cares for the lambs when they are hurt. God is our Shepherd. He loves and cares for us. He gives us everything we need. The promise of eternal life is the greatest gift the Shepherd has to offer.

Pray Today:

Read this psalm softly as your prayer.

Ten Commandments

January 8

Read the Bible:

Underline and read Exodus 20:3. Also underline
Psalm 103:2:
"Praise the Lord, O my soul, and forget not all his
benefits" (NIV).

Think About This:

When we like anything more than we love God, we
are worshiping that thing. The first commandment tells
us to worship and serve only God. Circle any of this list
that could become more important to you than God.

money   family
friends   jewelry
being popular   car
sports   traveling
beautiful clothing

Pray Today:

Pray: "Dear Heavenly Father, help me love and worship You. May nothing ever be so important to me that
I forget about You. In Jesus' name I pray. Amen."

January 9

Read the Bible:

Lightly color and read Exodus 20:4-6. Read and lightly color Psalm 100:2. "Serve the Lord with gladness: come before his presence with singing."

Think About This:

A missionary tells of visiting a small village and finding sticks, stones, and ugly clay images in front of the huts where the people lived. They were "graven images." When the people learned of Jesus, they removed the images.

We do not need images to worship God. We do not need "lucky charms." We have a loving Heavenly Father who cares for us.

Pray Today:

Ask God to help you depend on Him for everything you need. Pray that you will never use any kind of graven image but that you will love and serve God.

January 10

Read the Bible:

Underline and read Exodus 20:7 in your Bible.

Think About This:

What does using God's name "in vain" mean? It means anytime God's name is spoken in disrespect, His name is not being used properly. When people use God's name as they curse, they are using His name in vain. Sometimes people use God's name as slang. They call out God's name when they are not talking to Him. This is also using God's name in the wrong way.

Pray Today:

Ask God to help you think before you speak His name. Always respect and honor God's name. If others around you use His name dishonorably, ask them to please stop.

January 11

Read the Bible:

Lightly color or underline Exodus 20:8: "Remember the Sabbath day by keeping it holy" (NIV).
Underline and read Psalm 122:1.

Think About This:

We worship on Sunday because Jesus rose from the dead on the first day of the week. God made that day a very special day. We are to make that day a very special day too. How does God say that we are to keep this day holy?

You may want to read Exodus 20:9-11 to find the answer.

Pray Today:

Pray: "Dear God, help me worship you on Your day in ways that honor You because I love You. Amen."

January 12

Read the Bible:

Underline and read Exodus 20:12 and Ephesians 6:1.

Think About This:

Did you ever wonder why God made Adam and Eve grown-ups instead of children? Of course, children need parents to guide and teach them. God planned for children to honor and obey their parents.

You can honor your parents in many ways. Choose at least two from the list that you will do.

1. I will respect my parents by not talking back to them.

2. I will respect my parents by obeying the first time they ask me to do something.

3. I will respect my parents by telling them the truth.

4. I will respect my parents by being dependable.

5. I will honor my parents by thanking God for them.

Pray Today:

Thank God for your parents. Ask Him to help you honor and respect them.

January 13

Underline and read Exodus 20:13,15.
Psalm 101:2 says: "I will behave myself wisely."

Think About This:

God is the Giver of life. The Commandment in Exodus 20:13 tells us we should not kill. Every person is precious to God. We need to protect each other so that our lives can be lived for Christ.

The Commandment in verse 15 tells us not to take things that belong to others. Everything belongs to someone. When you are tempted to take something that you know you shouldn't, remember that God knows what we do even when no other person is around. God is not pleased when we steal. Practice being honest.

Pray Today:

Thank God for your life. Ask Him to help you respect the lives of others. If you have ever taken anything that did not belong to you, ask God to forgive you. Thank God for giving you the things you need. Ask God to help you live honestly.

January 14

Read the Bible:

Read and underline Exodus 20:14. Locate and underline Proverbs 3:5-6: "Trust in the Lord with all thine heart; and lean not unto thine own understanding. In all thy ways acknowledge him, and he shall direct thy paths."

Think About This:

God planned for families. He wanted families to live together and to love each other. He gave a Commandment that spoke against a husband or a wife living with someone other than the person they married. Everyone is happier when they live by God's rules.

Pray Today:

It will probably be many years before you marry, but you can begin to get ready for marriage by asking God now to help you marry the person He would choose for you. Ask God to give you a Christian home where all of you will love and serve God.

January 15

Read the Bible:

Underline and read Exodus 20:16 and 17. Find Psalm 19:14. Underline it. "May the words of my mouth and the meditation of my heart be pleasing in your sight, O Lord, my Rock and my Redeemer" (NIV).

Think About This:

Coveting often leads to stealing. When persons want something that belongs to others, they sometimes breaks two Commandments by coveting and stealing.

Telling something that is not true is "bearing false witness." Why do people tell lies? It may be because they are afraid that telling the truth will get them in trouble. Lying is wrong. It also can become a habit that is hard to break. Coveting can also become a habit. We see what others have and forget that God has given us many things.

Pray Today:

Pray: "Thank you, God, for everything You have given me. Help me not to want what other people have. Help me be careful of my thoughts and my words so that I will speak only those things that are true. In Jesus' name, amen."

Church

January 16

Read the Bible:

"He came to Nazareth, where he had been brought up: and, as his custom was, he went into the synagogue on the sabbath day, and stood up for to read" (Luke 4:16).

Think About This:

Jesus made a habit of going to church. It was a habit that His parents had helped Him form.

Worshiping with others should be a time of learning. It should be a time of praising and thanking God. It should be a happy time of sharing with family and friends.

Pray Today:

Pray that going to church will become a habit or "custom" that you will learn to enjoy and look forward to.

January 17

Read the Bible:

Read Acts 6:1-7

Think About This:

When the quarrel started over how the widows were treated, the apostles called the believers together. How did they solve the problem? _____

_____

How did they choose the men to be the special helpers or deacons? _____

Pray Today:

Pray for the deacons at your church. Ask God to help them as they care for those with needs.

January 18

Read the Bible:

Read Acts 2:42-47

"Day after day they met as a group in the Temple, and they had their meals together in their homes, eating with glad and humble hearts, praising God, and enjoying the good will of all the people. And every day the Lord added to their group those who were being saved" (Acts 2:46-47, GNB).

Think About This:

How is the church you just read about like your church? _____

Do the people of the church eat together?_____

Do they enjoy being together? _____

Do they praise God by singing and praying? _____

Pray Today:

Thank God for your church. Thank Him for special friends you have at church. Ask God to help you be friendly and caring to others in your church.

January 19

Read the Bible:

Find Matthew 28:19-20
"Go, then, to all peoples everywhere and make them my disciples: baptize them in the name of the Father, the Son, and the Holy Spirit, and teach them to obey everything I have commanded you. And I will be with you always, to the end of the age" (GNB).

Think About This:

The Scripture you have just read was one given to the disciples by Jesus. It is the message and the work of the church. People make up a church. We are to tell others of Jesus—that means the boys and girls next door or people in far away cities and continents.

Pray Today:

Pray for missionaries who are telling others of Jesus or helping in some way to make the gospel known to all people everywhere. Pray for your friends who worship with you at church. Pray that you will be able to share what you know about Jesus with someone.

January 20

Read the Bible:

Underline and read these verses in your Bible: Psalm 122:1; Ecclesiastes 5:1; and Psalm 100:4.

"When thou goest to the house of God, . . . be more ready to hear" (Ecclesiastes 5:1).

Think About This:

Be glad when you can go to church! When you worship God, it is a time to love and adore Him. It is a time to sing songs of praise! It is a time to think about the good things God has done for you. It is a time to listen to the music of the pianist or organist. It is a time to listen as the preacher tells about God.

Pray Today.

Thank God for your church. Thank god for your church family. Ask God to help you worship Him.

January 21

Read the Bible:

Locate and lightly color these verses in your Bible: Psalm 96:8; Psalm 100:4; and Matthew 21:13. Read them.

Think About This:

In Psalm 96:8 we read about bringing an offering and coming "into his courts." The best offering you could bring to Jesus would be your life.

In Psalm 100:4 we are told to enter His gates with thanksgiving and praise. What are you thankful for today? _____

What can you praise God for? Good health? A family who loves you? Friends? Food and clothing? Write other things you are thankful and can praise God for.

_____

Jesus said He wanted His "house" or church to be a place of prayer. Jesus wants men and women, boys and girls, to be reverent when they are in the house of the Lord.

Pray Today:

Praise or thank God for at least five things. Ask Him to help you go to church with the right attitude. Ask Him to help you be a worshiper who would not ever want to disturb others who have come to the "house of prayer."

January 22

Read the Bible:

Read Matthew 20:26-28 and Matthew 25:40.

Think About This:

Jesus often spoke of Himself as a servant or minister. He spent His days on earth helping people. Jesus healed the sick, taught people, cheered the lonely and sad, cared for sinners, fed the hungry, gave water to the thirsty, and loved the children. Helping others was a way of life. Jesus expects church people to help others.

How can you help others? Think of something you will do. Write it down.

Ask your parents to help you. Tell them what you want to do.

Pray Today:

Pray: "Dear God, You showed us how to live and help others. I would like to help someone today. Will You show me someone I can help? In Jesus' name, amen."

January 23

Read the Bible:

Find Acts in your Bible. Find chapter 2; then find verse 42. Carefully underline the verse.

Think About This:

The church plans activities to help the members grow and learn. Check the activities you have attended or taken part in.

___ Bible study   ___ Giving offering
___ Eating a fellowship meal   ___ Baptism
___ Praying   ___ Fellowships
___ Singing   ___ Lord's Supper
___ Worship service   ___ Mission activity
___ Deacon ordination   ___ Collecting food

Pray Today:

Pray: "Dear God, I thank You for my church. Thank You for all the activities that help me grow and learn of You. Help me want to serve You through the church all of my life. In Jesus' name I pray. Amen."

God

January 24

Read the Bible:

Underline Genesis 1:27 and Psalm 100:3 in your Bible.

"So God created human beings, making them to be like himself. He created them male and female" (GNB).

"Never forget that the Lord is God. He made us, and we belong to him; we are his people, we are his flock" (GNB).

Think About This:

God created the world and everything in it. His creations were good. His best creation was people. We human beings were made in the likeness of God. We are like God in being able to think, feel, decide things, plan, learn, work, talk, love, and serve. People are living souls, spiritual beings like God. We are able to worship and have fellowship with God.

Pray Today:

Look at God's world through a window. Enjoy all the beautiful things God made. Thank God for making you one of His creations. Name some people you are glad God made. Thank God for them.

January 25

Read the Bible:

Peter began to speak: "I now realize that it is true that God treats everyone on the same basis" (Acts 10: 34, GNB).

"This is what love is: it is not that we have loved God, but that he loved us and sent his Son to be the means by which our sins are forgiven" (1 John 4:10, GNB).

Underline these two verses in your Bible.

Think About This:

God made and loves all of the billions of people in the whole world. We may be divided into races and nationalities. We may speak different languages and have different colors of skin. But the marvelous truth is that no matter where persons live or what their race, God loves them. No matter how many people are born into the human race, each one is known and loved by God.

Pray Today:

Pray: "Dear God, thank You for making all different kinds of people. Help me love them all. Amen."

January 26

Read the Bible:

Read Luke 12:6-7; 22-31.
"The Lord thinketh upon me" (Psalm 40:17). Find and underline this verse in your Bible.

Think About This:

Jesus knew His friends worried about a lot of things. They worried for fear they would not have enough food to eat. They worried for fear they would not have enough clothes to wear. Jesus spoke to His friends saying, "God knows your needs, and He will care for you."

He told His friends that God even cares for the birds and what they eat and the flowers and how they grow. God loves you more than birds and flowers.

Pray Today:

Pray: "Thank you, God, for loving and caring for me. Help me not to worry. In Jesus' name, amen."

January 27

Read the Bible:

"O Lord my God, in thee do I put my trust" (Psalm 7:1).

"Blessed are all they that put their trust in thee" (Psalm 2:12).

Underline these two verses in your Bible.

Think About This:

Many Bible verses give us help in times of problems or discouragement. God can help us. We can trust Him to care about our problems.

Make a Bible marker out of a strip of construction paper or wide ribbon. Write on the marker a Bible verse to help when you have a problem:
- When afraid—Psalm 56:3
- When you don't like school—Ecclesiastes 9:10
- When brothers or sisters bother you—Philippians 2:14
- When you are tempted to steal—James 4:7

Pray Today:

Pray: "Heavenly Father, I know that I can trust You. Help me to trust You more and more. Amen."

January 28

Read the Bible:

Locate and lightly color these verses in your Bible.
"We are labourers together with God" (1 Corinthians 3:9).
"God is my helper. The Lord is my defender" (Psalm 54:4, GNB).

Think About This:

Have you ever tried to do a hard job by yourself? Have you ever had a hard job to do and had someone help you? Which way is the easiest?

God knows and cares when you have a hard job to do. God will help you when the job is too difficult, but you must ask for His help.

Pray Today:

Ask God to help you remember that you can always ask Him to help with a hard job.

January 29

Read the Bible:

Mark and remember this verse:
"We know that all things work together for good to them that love God, to them who are called according to his purpose" (Romans 8:28).

Think About This:

Sometimes things happen to us that may seem bad or unpleasant. God can use even unpleasant circumstances as a part of His plan.

Pray Today:

Pray: "Dear Heavenly Father, help me to see that You are always ready to help me—even when things seem really bad. I do love You and want to please You in all I do and say. In Jesus' name, amen."

January 30

Read the Bible:

"Be determined and confident. Do not be afraid of them. Your God, the Lord himself, will be with you. He will not fail you or abandon you" (Deuteronomy 31:6 GNB).

Think About This:

What makes you afraid? Is it people? New places you have to go? Tests at school? Jobs you have to do? Doing things in front of others?

Remember that God is with you wherever you go. He is with you whatever you have to do. He is with us even when we do wrong. He is ready to forgive. He will not fail you.

Pray Today:

Write a prayer to remind you that God is with you in any situation. Nothing is too hard for God.

January 31

Read the Bible:

Find James 1:17 in your Bible and fill in the blanks:
"Every _____ gift and every perfect _____ is
from _____, and cometh down from the _____."

"Thanks be unto God for his unspeakable gift" (2
Corinthians 9:15), "Let us thank God for his priceless
gift!" (GNB).

Think About This:

God has given us many good gifts, and one of His gifts
is priceless. The verses deal with how God showed His
love to us. What is the supreme expression of God's
love? If you are not sure of the answer to this question,
read John 3:16. If you know the verse, say it softly.

Pray Today:

Sing the "Doxology" or another praise song you
know as a prayer today. Thank God for all His gifts.
Thank Him especially for Jesus.

Obeying

February 1

Read the Bible:

Read Acts 5:14-29.
"Peter and the other apostles answered, "We must obey God, not men" (Acts 5:29, GNB).
We ought to obey God rather than men.

Think About This:

Who entered the Temple? _____
Who heard that the prison was empty? _____
Who was afraid of being stoned? _____
Why did the apostles obey God? _____

Pray Today:

Do you know anyone who does not want to hear about Jesus? Have you ever told anyone about Jesus? Ask God to help you tell someone about Jesus.

February 2

Read the Bible:

"Choose you this day whom ye will serve; . . . but as for me and my house, we will serve the Lord" (Joshua 24:15).

"Be ye doers of the word, and not hearers only" (James 1:22).

Can you find and read these verses from your Bible?

Think About This:

Many people study the Bible or attend church. They may know what God wants them to do. But knowing God's plan is only part of living the Christian life. God expects us to put into practice His plan for our lives. When we do His commandments, we choose to serve Him.

Pray Today:

Pray: "Dear God, help me show that I serve You by my actions. In Jesus' name, amen."

February 3

Read the Bible:

Find and color these verses in your Bible:
"Thou shalt do that which is right and good in the sight of the Lord" (Deuteronomy 6:18).
"Cease to do evil; Learn to do well" (Isaiah 1:16-17).

Think About This:

God can help you do what is right.
Make a list of problems or decisions which are bothering you.
 1.
 2.
 3.
Pray for those things you listed. Ask someone to pray with you about a particular problem.

Pray Today:

Go to a quiet place with the one you asked to pray with you. Each of you can pray out loud.

February 4

Read the Bible:

Read Matthew 7:24-27 in your Bible.
"Listen to my instruction and be wise; do not ignore it" (Proverbs 8:33, NIV).

Think About This:

Your Heavenly Father knows what is best for You. You can choose to obey Him. You can start now to make your life a gift to God.

Pray Today:

Pray: "Dear Heavenly Father, I want my life to be lived for You. I do not want to be like the foolish man who built his house on sand. Thank You for loving me and for helping me to make wise choices. In Jesus' name I pray. Amen."

February 5

Read the Bible:

Find John 13:35.
"If you have love for one another, then everyone will know that you are my disciples" (GNB).

Think About This:

God loved us first, and He expects us to love others. If we love others, people can tell we are followers of Jesus. Do you love those who love you? God wants us to love family members and friends.

Write on a card the name of a friend or family member. Write one reason you love that person. Share the card with the person whose name appears on the card.

Pray Today:

Use the card as a reminder to pray for the person you named.

February 6

Read the Bible:

Locate and underline these Bible verses:
"If you love me, you will obey my commandments"
(John 14:15, GNB).
"We must obey God, not men" (Acts 5:29, GNB).

Think About This:

Make a list of commandments that God has given you
to obey.
1.
2.
3.
4.
5.
6.

Is it easy to obey God? What can you do to help you
obey God?

Pray Today:

Pray that you will obey God because you love Him.

February 7

Read the Bible:

"Obey them that have the rule over you" (Hebrews 13:17).
"Hear instruction, and be wise" (Proverbs 8:33).

Think About This:

One way we can show God we love Him is to obey Him.
What does obedience mean?

When is it difficult to do right?

What Bible verses can you learn and remember when you are tempted to disobey God's teachings?

Locate and underline these Bible verses. Memorize at least one of them.
When tempted to disobey God: John 14:15.
When tempted not to study: Isaiah 1:17.
When tempted to disobey health laws: Daniel 1:8.
When tempted to use bad words: Psalm 19:14.
When tempted to break laws: Proverbs 20:11.

Pray Today:

Pray: "Dear God, help me choose to obey Your rules. Help me to remember Bible verses when I am tempted to disobey. In Jesus' name, amen."

Love

February 8

Read the Bible:

Read 1 Cornthians 13:5-7. Lightly color these verses.
"Love is not ill-mannered or selfish or irritable; love does not keep a record of wrongs; love is not happy with evil, but is happy with the truth (GNB).

Think About This:

Bill's friend always wanted to choose the games to play. He wanted to be first every time. If Bill ever did anything wrong, his friend reminded him of it over and over.

Bill found some new friends. Bill's old friend wondered why Bill did not have time to play with him any more.

Have you ever been like Bill's friend? Have you ever realized you were being selfish and then asked God to forgive you? Did you tell your friend you were sorry?

Pray Today:

Pray: "Heavenly Father, please help me to be a good friend to others. Help me love them enough to not hold a grudge or remind them of things they have done wrong. Help me to be careful what I say about others. Amen."

February 9

Read the Bible:

Read John 3:1-21.
"For God loved the world so much that he gave his only Son, so that everyone who believes in him may not die but have eternal life" (v. 16, GNB).

Think About This:

After reading the story in John 3, decide if these statements are true or false.

Nicodemus understood everything Jesus said. True or false.

Being "born again" means choosing Jesus as your Savior. True or false.

God loves everyone in the world. True or false.

"The light" is talking about Jesus. True or false.

Pray Today:

Thank God for loving you. Ask Him to help you act in ways that are pleasing to Him.

February 10

Read the Bible:

Read Mark 12:30-31. Underline the verses in your Bible. [You must] " 'Love the Lord your God with all your heart, with all your soul, and with all your mind, and with all your strength.' The second most important commandment is this: '[You must] Love your neighbor as you love yourself.' There is no other commandment more important than these two" (GNB).

Think About This:

What four ways did Jesus say we must love God?

Jesus knew these two great commandments because He learned them as a child. You can find them in the Old Testament: Deuteronomy 6:5; Leviticus 19:18*b*.

Do you remember the story Jesus to told when the man asked the question: "Who is my neighbor?" Read that favorite story of the good Samaritan in the Gospel of Luke 10:25-37. God's love helps us do things for others in Jesus' name.

Pray Today:

Pray: "Heavenly Father, I want to put You first in my life. Help me love people the way Jesus loved them. Amen."

February 11

Read the Bible:

Lightly color this verse in your Bible: 1 John 3:18.
"My children! Our love should not be just words and talk; it must be true love, which shows itself in action" (GNB).

Think About This:

Can you think of some times when you said you would do something and then you failed to do it? Love is not just saying you will do something! Love means you will try hard to do what you promise to do.

Nehemiah wanted to help the people rebuild the walls around Jerusalem. Nehemiah prayed, and God let him go to Jerusalem and lead the people in rebuilding the walls. Nehemiah also led the people to return to worshiping and obeying God. Nehemiah's love was more than words.

Pray Today:

Ask God to help you show your love by the things you do as well as by the things you say.

February 12

Read the Bible:

Lightly color this verse in the Book of Deuteronomy: 15:11.

"Thou shalt open thine hand wide unto they brother, to thy poor, and to thy needy."

Think About This:

One church takes an offering on Wednesday night that is called the "Open Hand Offering." People are asked to "reach into their pockets and purses and give an offering." The money is given freely. No names are attached to the givers' offering. It is an offering given in Jesus' name to help those in need.

Pray Today:

You can decide now to share what you have with God. Pray: "Father, while I am still young I want to decide to share what You have blessed me with to help others. Guide me to choose the kind of work you want me to do. Help me to show love to others by helping when there is a need. Amen."

February 13

Read the Bible:

Read John 11:55-57; 12:12-13.
"This is what love is: it is not that we have loved God, but that he loved us and sent his son to be the means by which our sins are forgiven" (1 John 4:10, GNB).

Think About This:

How did the people greet Jesus as He came into Jerusalem?

It was just a few days later that Jesus was crucified. Do you suppose any of these same people were in the crowd that just a few days later screamed, "Crucify Him!"?

Pray Today:

Think about how Jesus showed His love. Ask God to help you show His love to others.

February 14

Read the Bible:

Read John 13:1-5; 21-30.

Think About This:

It was the custom in Bible times to wash the feet of a guest. Do you know why Jesus washed the disciples' feet? He was trying to show them that He not only loved them but also was willing to be a servant.

Pray Today:

Thank God for letting Jesus show us how to love others.

Promises

February 15

Read the Bible:

Find and underline Isaiah 65:24 and Matthew 7:7.
"Before they call, I will answer; and while they are still speaking, I will hear" (NIV).
"Ask, and you will receive; seek, and you will find; knock, and the door will be opened to you" (GNB).

Think About This:

God makes many promises to us. One of the best promises is that He will hear us when we pray. Isn't is wonderful to know that even before we finish praying, God is hearing and caring and loving us?

Pray Today:

Pray: "Heavenly Father, thank You for listening to me when I talk to You. Help me feel You near. Help me ask for things that are pleasing to You. Forgive me when I forget to talk to You. I love You and want to be obedient to You. Thank You for the Bible. In Jesus' name, amen"

February 16

Read the Bible:

Lightly color Isaiah 46:4 in your Bible. "I am your God and will take care of you until you are old and your hair is gray. I made you and will care for you; I will give you help and rescue you" (GNB).

Think About This:

God has promised that He will always take care of each of us. How long does the verse in Isaiah say He will care for us?

Your hair will not turn gray for many years. As long as you live, God will love and care for you and help you with any problems you may have. Isn't that a wonderful promise?

Have you thought about a promise you could make to God? Think about it and then fill in the sentence.

Because I love You and want to serve You, I promise to try to _____. Print your initials by the promise.

Pray Today:

Ask God to help you keep your promise to Him.

February 17

Read the Bible:

Lightly color Psalm 4:8 and Hebrews 13:6.

Think About This:

Have you ever been afraid? Do you feel safe when your parents are near? Your Heavenly Father is always close to you. You are never alone because God is always with you.

Katy had to stay with friends while her mother was in the hospital. Her friends taught her a song with these words: "What time I am afraid, I will put my trust in Thee" Katy sang the song many times. One day she told her friends, "I believe the words to that song. I can truthfully say I am not afraid!"

Pray Today:

Pray: "Dear God, help me remember the Bible verses in Psalms and Hebrews the next time I am afraid. Thank You for promising to be with me when I am afraid. In Jesus' name, amen."

February 18

Read the Bible:

Read and underline these Bible verses:
• Psalm 86:5
• Luke 6:37
• Luke 23:34

Think About This:

In Psalm 86:5, the psalmist says, "Thou, Lord, art good and ready to _____.

Luke 6:37 says: "_____, and ye shall be _____.

Jesus said as He was being crucified, "Father, _____ them (Luke 23:34).

God is always ready to forgive us when we ask Him. This is another of His good promises.

Pray Today:

Begin by asking God to forgive you for anything you have done wrong. Is there someone you have been mad at whom you need to forgive? Can you tell that person that you forgive them?

Thank God for His promise of forgiveness.

February 19

Read the Bible:

Read and lightly color John 14:1-4.

Think About This:

Jesus promised four things in the first four verses of John 14:

1. The Heavenly Father has many mansions.
2. Jesus said He was preparing a place for us.
3. Jesus promised to come again to earth.
4. Jesus promised we could be with Him.

For everyone who chooses Christ as Savior, these four promises are very precious. Heaven is a wonderful place that God has planned for those who love and honor Him.

Pray Today:

Thank God for the promises found in John 14. Thank God for the Bible.

February 20

Read the Bible:

Underline John 14:16-19.
"I will ask the Father, and he will give you another Helper, who will stay with you forever. He is the Spirit, who reveals the truth about God. The world cannot receive him, because it cannot see him or know him. But you know him, because he remains with you and is in you" (GNB).

Think About This:

When Jesus knew that He was going back to Heaven, He gave a promise that you read in John 14:16-17. That promise was the Holy Spirit who helps us know that Jesus is truly the Son of God. The Holy Spirit is the One who helps us know that we need to accept Jesus as our Savior.

Pray Today:

Pray: "Heavenly Father, thank You for sending your Holy Spirit to be with us. Thank You for loving us enough to not leave us all alone. Help us obey you when the Holy Spirit makes us think of things we should do. In Jesus' name, amen."

February 21

Read the Bible:

Read carefully and underline these Bible verses:
John 5:24; Luke 19:10; Romans 6:23.

Think About This:

God has promised eternal life for those who trust
Jesus Christ as their Savior. Christians do not have to
worry what will happen to them when they die. Those
who trust their lives to Jesus Christ—who believe that
He died on the cross for their sins—will spend eternity
in heaven with God.

Pray Today:

Thank God for the promise of heaven to all those
who trust in Him. If you have not asked Jesus to come
into your life, ask Him to help you understand the Bible
so that you can decide to become a Christian.

Getting Along

February 22

Read the Bible:

Read and underline Romans 14:19 in your Bible.

"So then, we must always aim at those things that bring peace and that help strengthen one another" (GNB).

Think About This:

Why do people fight? List three ways you could settle a disagreement without fighting.

1.
2.
3.

Pray Today:

Pray that you will want to be a peacemaker. Ask God to help you use your mind to think of ways to stay at peace with your family and friends.

February 23

Read the Bible:

Read and underline Psalm 133:1 in your Bible.

Think About This:

Do you remember the story of Abraham and Lot? Abraham did not want his servants and Lot's herdsmen fighting over the grass and water. Abraham suggested that Lot choose which part of the land he wanted for his herdsmen. Abraham wanted God to be pleased with him. He knew that quarreling was not a happy way to live. God blessed Abraham. God will bless you when you refuse to quarrel with people in your family and community.

Pray Today:

Pray: "Dear God, help me get along with others in my family. Help me do my part to make our home a happy place to be. Amen."

February 24

Read the Bible:

Read Genesis 26:1-25.
"Blessed are the peacemakers: for they shall be called the children of God" (Matthew 5:9).

Think About This:

How did God bless Isaac when he planted grain?

Why did Abimelech tell Isaac to leave?

What did Isaac do?

How did Isaac show that he worshiped God?

Pray Today:

Ask God to forgive you for times when you have quarreled. Ask Him to help you to be a peacemaker.

February 25

Read the Bible:

Find 1 John 4:7 in your Bible. Read the verse carefully. Think about it for a few moments. Now think about your family. Read the verse once more.

"Beloved, let us love one another, for love is from God; and everyone who loves is born of God and knows God" (NASB).

Think About This:

Sometimes brothers and sisters have a hard time showing love for each other. God planned for families to love and care for each other. Everyone in a family doing their part makes a happy home. Write each family member's name on a sheet of paper. List one thing you will do today to show each person that you love him or her. When you have completed each thing you have chosen to do, put a check mark by that person's name.

Pray Today:

Thank God for the people in your family. Ask God to help you be loving and kind to each person in your family.

February 26

Read the Bible:

Find Proverbs 15:1 in your Bible. Lightly color the verse after you have read it. "A gentle answer quiets anger, but a harsh one stirs it up" (GNB).

Think About This:

When you get mad and yell or argue with someone, what do they do? Most of the time that person yells back at you. Someone must change the angry feelings by being quiet and trying to be calm and gentle.

It is hard to yell at someone who answers you quietly. When you get angry today, try to stay calm and talk in a soft voice. Practice controlling your temper.

Pray Today:

Pray: "Dear Heavenly Father, help me express my anger in a calm way. In Jesus' name, amen."

February 27

Read the Bible:

Underline James 5:16 in your Bible. "Confess your faults one to another, and pray one for another, that ye may be healed. The effectual fervent prayer of a righteous man availeth much."

Think About This:

What is a fault? A fault is a sin or a bad habit. Some boys and girls have a bad habit (sin) of cheating on tests or games. Others may have the fault (sin) of saying unkind things about others. Some people may have the fault (sin) of lying.

A righteous person is a person who does things God's way. James said that the prayer of a righteous person brings good results.

Think of people you need to pray for. Someone who:
has a problem _____
has a bad habit _____
has trouble getting along with others _____
is sick or unhappy _____

Pray Today:

Ask God to help you get along with others by praying for them. Do you need to pray for yourself?

February 28

Read the Bible:

Lightly color Ephesians 4:32. "Instead, be kind and tender-hearted to one another, and forgive one another, as God has forgiven you through Christ" (GNB).

Think About This:

The first part of this Bible verse, "Be ye kind," may be the first Bible verse you learned as a little child.

Think of ways you can be kind to others including friends, family, schoolmates, and neighbors. Can you listen when someone else speaks? Can you let others be first? Can you take turns? Can you forgive someone who has been unkind to you? Can you say *please* and *thank you?*

Pray Today:

Pray: "Dear God, I know that I am not always kind. Please help me be kind to my family and my friends. Help me treat others the way Jesus treated people. In Jesus' name I pray. Amen."

Jesus

March 1

Read the Bible:

Read John 1:1-4. Now read it here with the word *Jesus* printed instead of "the Word."

In the beginning was Jesus, and Jesus was with God, and Jesus was God. The same was in the beginning with God. All things were made by him; and without him was not any thing made that was made. In him was life; and the life was the light of men.

Think About This:

How does the first chapter of Genesis begin?

What do the verses in John 1 tell you about Jesus?

What do they tell you about God? What is God like?

Pray Today:

Thank God for Jesus. Thank God for faith to believe the Bible. Thank God for letting you be a part of the world.

March 2

Read Luke 2:41-52.

" 'Son, why have you done this to us? Your father and I have been terribly worried trying to find you.' He answered them, 'Why did you have to look for me? Didn't you know that I had to be in my Father's house?' " (v.v. 48-49, GNB).

Think About This:

Jesus wanted to be in the Temple, His Father's house. He was eager to learn. The Bible says He listened to the teachers and asked them questions.

When you go to church, do you go to listen and learn?

Pray Today:

Pray: "Dear Father, help me want to go to church. Help me listen to my teachers. Help me learn everything I can about Jesus and the things He taught. Amen."

March 3

Read the Bible:

Read about Jesus being baptized in Matthew 3:13-17. Underline verse 17: "Then a voice said from heaven, 'This is my own dear Son, with whom I am pleased' " (GNB).

Think About This:

Jesus told John the Baptist that He was being baptized in obedience to God (v. 15). People are baptized today for the same reason—to show obedience to God. It also shows people attending the baptism that the new Christians are not ashamed to be baptized in the name of Jesus.

Baptism is a very special time in the life of a believer.

Pray Today:

Thank God for the example Jesus set. Pray for anyone you have seen baptized recently.

March 4

Read the Bible:

Read Mark 1:14-20. Lightly color verses 16 and 17.
"As Jesus walked along the shore of Lake Galilee, He
saw two fishermen, Simon and his brother Andrew,
catching fish with a net. Jesus said to them, 'Come with
me, and I will teach you to catch men' " (GNB).

Think About This:

Jesus recognized that He would need help. He en-
listed twelve men to be His disciples. God wants us to
tell others about Jesus. Jesus taught His disciples for
more than three years. Go to Sunday School and worship services as often as you can. Share with your
friends what you learn about Jesus.

Pray Today:

Pray: "Heavenly Father, help me listen and learn
from my pastor and teachers. Help me tell my friends
how much Jesus loves them. In Jesus' name, amen."

March 5

Read the Bible:

Read and underline John 20:31.

Think About This:

Jesus healed people. He loved people whom no one else loved. Jesus took time to talk to people. The four Gospels record many stories of Jesus showing love to others. The Gospel of John says that the reason these things are written is so "that you may believe that Jesus is the Messiah, the Son of God, and that through your faith in him you may have life" (GNB).

Pray Today:

Ask God to help you really believe that Jesus is the Son of God. Thank Him for the many ways He shows His love to you.

March 6

Read the Bible:

Read Matthew 15:29-31.
"We love because God first loved us" (1 John 4:19, GNB).

Think About This:

Jesus loved people. He showed His love in many ways. He talked to Nicodemus. He loved Zacchaeus when no one else seemed to. He felt sad when people were sick. He made them well. He wanted people to love and honor God. He told many stories about how people should live and how we should treat each other. Jesus loved people.

Pray Today:

Thank God for Jesus' love.

March 7

Read the Bible:

Read John 9:1-12.
"While I am in the world, I am the light for the world" (John 9:5, GNB).

Think About This:

People in Old Testament times, New Testament times, and some people today feel that all sickness is a result of sin. Jesus said this was not so. When He healed this blind man, many people who had known the blind man all of his life asked many questions.

Pray Today:

Pray: "Thank You, God, for Jesus. Thank You for caring about me when I am sick. Help me take care of my body. In Jesus' name, amen."

March 8

Read the Bible:

Finish reading the story of the blind man whom Jesus healed. Read John 9:13-38.

" 'I believe, Lord!' the man said, and knelt down before Jesus" (John 9:38, GNB).

Think About This:

What questions did the Pharisees ask the man who had been healed?

What questions did they ask his parents?

Why did Jesus go find the man?

Pray Today:

Thank God for caring about people who need help

Missions

March 9

Read the Bible:

Find and lightly color Acts 1:8. Read the verse.

Think About This:

After Jesus' resurrection and before He went back to heaven, Jesus gave the disciples some special instructions to follow. Reread Acts 1:8. Did you hear the three directions Jesus gave the disciples? What were they?

1.
2.
3.

How can you carry out Jesus' command today?

Pray Today:

Thank God for the privilege of telling others about Jesus.

March 10

Read the Bible:

"Go home to thy friends, and tell them how great things the Lord hath done for thee" (Mark 5:19). Locate and underline that verse.

Think About This:

This Bible verse explains how a person can witness or testify about Jesus. Who do you know who needs to hear about Jesus? _____ and _____

On a separate piece of paper, make a list of the great things God has done for you. Share your list.

Pray Today:

Ask God to help you share the good news of Jesus with someone today.

March 11

Read the Bible:

Find and read slowly and carefully John 3:16.

Think About This:

God loves you. Read the verse again and replace the words "the world" with your name.

What are some ways to show God's love?

Make a Bible verse puzzle. Write John 3:16 on a sheet of paper. Cut the sheet into puzzle pieces. Put the pieces in an envelope. Share the puzzle with someone who needs to know John 3:16.

Pray Today:

Pray: "Thank You, God, for Your love to me. Amen."

March 12

Read the Bible:

Read and lightly color John 1:40-42.

Think About This:

Andrew and Peter were brothers. The Bible tells more about Peter than it does Andrew. But Andrew brought Peter to Jesus.

We are responsible to help our family members know God's love. Does everyone in your family love God? Is everyone in your family a Christian?

Pray Today:

Ask God to bless your family members. Call each one by name as you pray.

March 13

Read the Bible:

Read Romans 10:13-15 in your Bible.

Think About This:

What do these verses mean to you?

Find another translation of the Bible and read this passage.
Rewrite the verses in your own words. Share your version of the passage with someone.

If you told someone about Jesus, what would you tell? Write down five facts you know about Jesus.
1.
2.
3.
4.
5.

Pray Today:

Ask God to help you share the message of His love with someone today.

March 14

Read the Bible:

Read the story found in Acts 8:26-39.

Think About This:

Philip met a man from Ethiopia who was reading from the Scriptures. Because the man did not understand what he was reading, Philip explained the good news about Jesus.

Many people want and need to know about God's love. You may be the only child to tell another child about Jesus.

Pray Today:

Ask God to help you be brave enough to tell another child about Jesus.

March 15

Read the Bible:

Locate and lightly color 1 John 4:14.
"We have seen and do testify that the Father sent the Son to be the Saviour of the world."

Think About This:

Missionaries and preachers are not the only Christians who are to tell others about God's love. All of us who know Jesus should tell others about Him.

Make a stand-up card for the table. Use a large card or thick paper folded in the middle to stand up. Copy 1 John 4:14 on the card. Write the names of two friends whom you need to tell about Jesus.

Pray Today:

Pray for your two friends who need to hear about Jesus.

Myself

March 16

Read the Bible:

Find, underline, and read Deuteronomy 6:18 and 3 John 11.

"Dear friend, do not imitate what is evil but what is good" (NIV).

Think About This:

You are free to make some choices. Is it always easy to make good choices? Of course not! You will grow stronger each time you make a right choice.

Listed below are some choices you may need to make this week. Think about how you will handle them. Will you choose to do some of them? Put a * by those you already know would be a good choice.

- Take a shower or a bath.
- Obey teachers at school.
- Make fun of someone at school or church.
- Watch TV late at night.
- Try smoking a cigarette.
- Help a family member with some work.
- Read your Bible each day.

Pray Today:

Thank God that you can choose to obey Him.

March 17

Read the Bible:

Locate and lightly color or underline these three Bible verses: Romans 12:10; Galatians 6:10; and Mark 12:31. Read all three verses.

Think About This:

God planned for friends. He also planned how you should treat your friends. God made us all different but able to appreciate others who are different from us.

Get a piece of paper. Write on it the name of one of your friends. Beside the friend's name write some words that describe that friend.

Pray Today:

Pray for your friend. Pray for other friends. Call them by name, asking God to help you love your friends as you should.

March 18

Read the Bible:

Read Mark 10:13-16 from your Bible. Lightly underline this short story.

Think About This:

The words to a children's song tell this story:
Jesus loves the children,
Held them on His knee.
Placed His hands on each one's head,
Took them in His arms and said,
"Let the little children come to me."

Pray Today:

Thank God for loving you. You are very special to God.

March 19

Read the Bible:

Underline or lightly color 1 Peter 5:7 in your Bible. Read the verse.

Think About This:

Isn't it good to know that there are people who care for you? Parents show their love by taking care of you. How long has it been since you thanked your mom or dad for preparing food for you, keeping your clothes clean, or taking care of you when you were hurt or sick?

Have you ever felt like no one cared for you? God does. He knows your name. He knows all about you. He cares for you.

Pray Today:

Thank God for family members who care for your needs and so show that they care for you. Thank God for listening to you when you pray.

March 20

Read the Bible:

Read 1 Samuel 16; 17:12-22.
"Whoever is faithful in small matters will be faithful in large ones; whoever is dishonest in small matters will be dishonest in large ones" (Luke 16:10, GNB).

Think About This:

David was a dependable. Name a job you can be depended upon to do in your home. _____ If you are given a job to do that you do not like very much, can you be dependable? Will you do your best?

Pray Today:

Ask God to help you be dependable in both small and big jobs that you have to do today.

March 21

Read the Bible:

"For it is by God's grace that you have been saved through faith. It is not the result of your own efforts, but God's gift, so that no one can boast about it. God has made us what we are, and in our union with Christ Jesus he has created us for a life of good deeds, which he has already prepared for us to do" (Ephesians 2:8-10, GNB).

Think About This:

Your life and the things you do are your gift to Christ. The things you do will not earn a place in heaven for you. Jesus' death on the cross provides that. If our good deeds saved us, we could brag about them, but that was not God's good plan.

Pray Today:

Pray today that God will help you live your life as a gift to Him.

March 22

Read the Bible:

Underline this verse in your Bible:
"Jesus increased in wisdom and stature, and in favour with God and man" (Luke 2:52).

Think About This:

Jesus learned from His parents. He learned from the synagogue school. He grew wiser. He ate good food. He grew taller and stronger in His body. He acted in such a way that people were pleased with Him and God was pleased with Him.

Pray Today:

You may want to pray this prayer: "Dear God, help me do my best at school. Help me know that I can learn from my parents and teachers. Help me choose to eat foods that will make my body strong and healthy. Help me act today so that my family and friends will be pleased and that You will also be pleased by the things I say and do. In Jesus' name I pray. Amen."

March 23

Read the Bible:

Read Exodus 3:1-10. This is the story of God talking to Moses. Find and underline Philippians 4:13. "I can do all things through Christ which strengtheneth me."

Think About This:

Do you realize you can do many things? On a piece of paper, make a list of things you do well. (Math, reading, singing, finishing a job, memorizing Bible verses.)

Are there some things you find hard to do?

Moses thought he could not do what God wanted him to do. God gave Moses the ability to do a hard job. He asked Moses to go back to Egypt and lead the slaves to a new land! That was a big job!

God has given you abilities and talents to do many things. You can learn to do many other things. When you have a hard job to do, it is better to ask God to help you than to make excuses and not try at all.

Pray Today:

Thank God for helping you when you have hard things to do. Ask Him to help you to be willing to do difficult things. Thank God for giving you the strength you need to finish a job you start.

People

March 24

Read the Bible:

Read Luke 5:17-26. "Serve one another in love" (Galatians 5:13, NIV).

Think About This:

Did you ever decide to help someone and then it just seemed like too much trouble? What problem did the men in the story have when they wanted to help their friend?

Finish these sentences:

A good friend will help when _____.

When the Bible says, "By love serve one another," it means that you will _____.

When several friends get together to do a job, it takes _____.

Pray Today:

Pray: "Dear Heavenly Father, please help me to work with my friends when there is a hard job to do. Help me not to be bossy or have to have my way. Give me some ideas on how I can help others in Jesus' name. Thank You for my friends. In Jesus' name I pray. Amen."

March 25

Read the Bible:

Locate and read Jeremiah 38:1-13. "My lord the king, these men have acted wickedly in all they have done to Jeremiah the prophet. They have thrown him into a cistern, where he will starve to death when there is no longer any bread in the city" (v. 9, NIV).

Think About This:

Ebedmelech saved Jeremiah's life. He was a slave or servant of the king. His people had a reputation for being cruel. What do you suppose made Ebedmelech different?

How did Ebedmelech help Jeremiah?

Have you ever had a problem and needed help? Have you ever helped anyone who was in trouble? How did you feel after you helped the person?

Pray Today:

Thank God for the Bible stories of people like Ebedmelech. Ask God to help you watch for times when you can help others.

March 26

Read the Bible:

Read and underline Luke 16:10. "Whoever is faithful in small matters will be faithful in large ones; whoever is dishonest in small matters will be dishonest in large ones" (GNB).

Think About This:

Rhoda was a little servant girl who lived in the home of Mary. Mary was the mother of Mark. Peter, their friend was in prison. His friends were at Mary's home praying that Peter would be released.

We do not know how old Rhoda was, but she may have been your age. Late at night Rhoda heard someone knocking on the door. When she heard Peter's voice, she was so excited she forgot to let him in. Instead, she ran to tell the others who were still praying for Peter to get out of prison!

This story is found in Acts 12:1-19.

What did the people say to Rhoda when she told them Peter was at the door?

What did Peter do?

Pray Today:

Ask God to help you do small jobs well so that He can depend on you to do big jobs too.

March 27

Read the Bible:

Find and underline Psalm 144:15. "Happy are the people whose God is the Lord!" (GNB).

Think About This:

Do you know the story of Nehemiah? Do you remember that he wanted to rebuild the walls of Jerusalem? Nehemiah asked the people to help him. Many, many people helped. Some did not do their share, and others did more than their share.

Read Nehemiah 3:12. Shallum, ruler of half of Jerusalem, helped build the wall. Who helped Shallum? Are you surprised?

God has work for both boys and girls. When there is work to be done, God uses those who are willing. Ask God to help you choose a vocation or job.

Pray Today:

Pray: "Dear God, help me do whatever work You need done. Help me study and prepare to be whatever You want me to be. In Jesus' name, amen."

March 28

Read the Bible:

Can you find the book of Philemon? It is just one chapter. It is right before Hebrews. Lightly color verse 7. "Your love has given me great joy and encouragement, because you, brother, have refreshed the hearts of the saints" (NIV).

Think About This:

Philemon was Paul's friend. In fact, Paul had told Philemon about Jesus. Philemon became a Christian. Onesimus was a slave. He had run away from Philemon. A master could kill a slave who ran away.

Onesimus also heard about Jesus from Paul. He, too, accepted Christ. Paul sent the slave home but asked his friend to treat the slave as a fellow Christian.

Have you ever done something wrong and someone helped you? What do you think Philemon did when he read the letter from Paul?

Pray Today:

Ask God to help you be a friend to new people who come to your church.

March 29

Read the Bible:

Read Psalm 8. Choose a favorite verse to lightly color.

Think About This:

Through the years people have written songs to be used to worship God. When songs people sing are put together in a book it is called a hymnal. The Book of Psalms is a book of songs in the Bible. It is a collection of songs Jewish people often sang as they worshiped. King David wrote many of the songs (psalms.)

One song David wrote is Psalm 8. David praised God because he knew God was so great.

Pray Today:

Write a praise song as a prayer thanking God for His greatness.

March 30

Read the Bible:

Read John 6:1-14.

Think About This:

Jesus needed what the lad had to share. Think about and answer the following questions:

• What do you suppose the boy thought when he was asked to share his lunch?

• How do you think the boy felt when Jesus thanked God for the food?

• Were other people helped because the boy shared his lunch?

• Think of times when others were helped because of a right choice you made?

Pray Today:

Ask God to help you make right choices when you have opportunities to share and help others.

March 31

Read the Bible:

Read Acts 9:36-43.

"In Joppa there was a woman named Tabitha, who was a believer. (Her name in Greek is Dorcas, meaning "a deer.") She spent all her time doing good" (Acts 9:36, GNB).

Think About This:

A lot of facts are not known about Dorcas. What we do know is that Dorcas was busy doing good things for others. What a wonderful way to think of someone!

Think of someone in your home or church who spends his or her time helping others.

Pray Today:

Thank God for people who spend their time helping others. Ask God to help you want to do good things for others.